*This book is dedicated to
everyone whose creativity and
imagination made it possible.*

What is a 'simple pleasure'?

*This was the question we asked **Baileys**® lovers early in 2006. We wanted to know what else made them happy, so we asked them to send us their 'simple pleasure' on a postcard.*

At the time we had no idea how many people would take part, and could hardly believe our eyes when we were inundated with thousands of mini masterpieces. We felt we just had to share them with the world. So here it is, a little book full of simple pleasures.

To everyone who contributed – those who made it into the book and those who we simply couldn't fit in – thank you so much.

*Making this book has been a pleasure for all of us at **The Baileys**® **Lounge**. We hope you enjoy it as much as we do.*

Amy Slack, Altrincham

Closing my eyes whilst someone counts my freckles! It's SO relaxing!

Rebecca Dainton, Lawrence Weston

Anonymous, Wembley

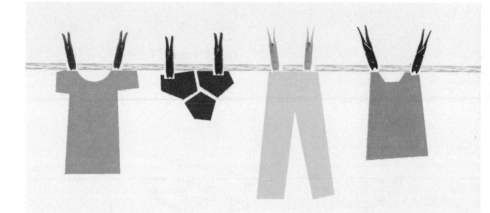

*My washing line full with Pegs matching
the clothes they are attached to*

Sharon Goddard, Braintree

Paula Harbour, Stubbington

Mrs Wilkins, St. Leonards on Sea

Being real
and being Surrounded
by real
People !!!

Fake is so over

Ronnie Curtin, London

I LOVE LISTENING TO ELVIS PRESLEY CD'S

Nia Jones, Gwynedd

Wrapping Presents

I love to drape curly strips
of silver & gold,
purple & blue. A
ribbon or bow finishes off,
so before you rip & tear,
take a moment to look and
stare, a gift wrapped in care

Helen Griffin, Somerset

Joanne Simmons, Cleethorpes

Joyce Hobbs, Hempstead

Tracey Glenn, Northampton

Emma Inch, Aberdeen

Lynn Snape, West Midlands

Frances Moore, Keswick

my
big
slide

Heather Korbey, Nailsworth

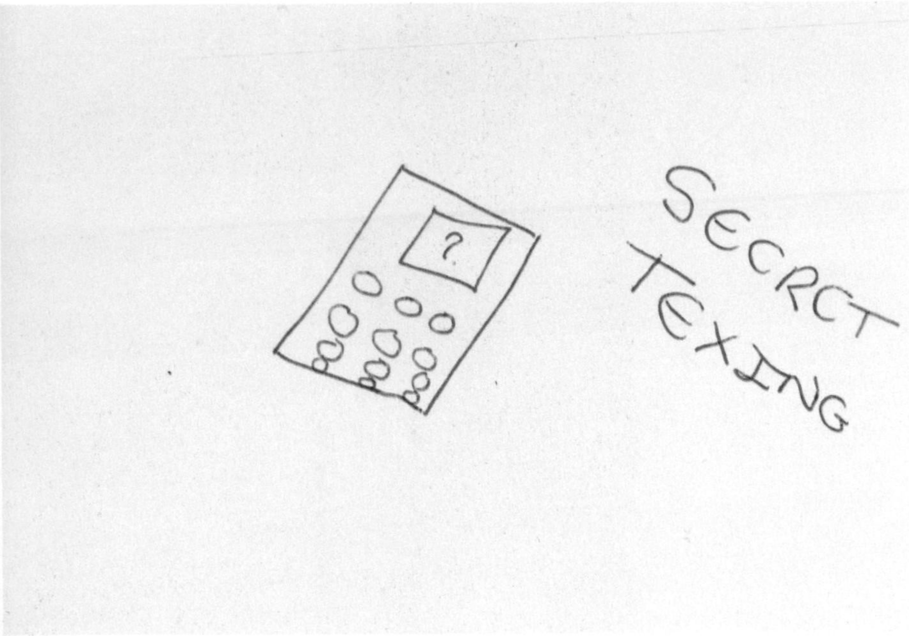

SECRCT TEXING

Abi Tugwood, Basildon

Nina Pearson, Sheffield

LEARNING THAX EX'S ARE LIKE. FUNGUS, THEY KEEP COMING BACK

Dawn Newman, Haywards Heath

Jennifer Creese, Southampton

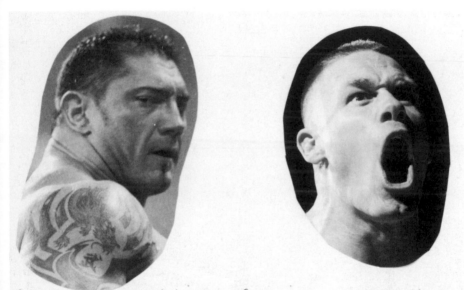

Relaxing whilst watching my favourite WWE wrestlers
i wishing i could join in on a match!!!

Sarah Parker, Mansfield

Helene Turner, Bedfordshire

Sara Miller, Auchterarder

4 BRICK SOLID WALLS

Michaela McNeely, Milton Keynes

Sarah Payne, Newport

Jemma Harnson, Northwich

Buying (and wearing) Naughty Undies!!

Nicola Bradley, West Midlands

Wearing new socks!

Mrs Hardwick, Chesterfield

B. Englund, Kent

Hearing the waves of the ocean wash over the pebbles on the beach

Sarah Whiteley, Sheffield

Maria Leatham, Oxford

Gemma Sullivan, Cornwall

SHOPPING!

Emma Pooley, Suffolk

Nicola Thomas, Gunthorpe

My simple pleasure is running my fingers through my lovely new thick curly hair! It has returned brand new after Chemo !!!

P.S. Sorry I can't spare you any

Cynthia Stewart, Whitby

Jenny Davies, Gravesend

I WOULD LOVE TO HAVE MORE £ SO
I COULD PAY OF MY 🏠 AND MAYBE
BUY A NEW. 🚗 BUT UNLESS I
WIN THE 🎗 ITS NOT GOING TO
HAPPEN! AND WOULD'NT IT BE GREAT
TO ✈ TO A NICE ☀ BEACH AS
I HAVE'NT BEEN ABROAD SINCE I
GOT 👫 AND THATS BEEN 7 YEARS
NOW! ATLEAST I HAVE A LONELY
👶♀ AND A FAT BLACK 🐱
AND NOT FORGETTING GOOD
HEALTH AND THE ❤ OF A
GORGEOUS ♂!

MAYBE THATS ALL I NEED TO—

Lisa Glen, Arbroath

Stacey Elford, Barnstaple

Veronica Fegan, Middlesbrough

My heated car seat on a cold morning

Anonymous, Cornwall

Knowing I Have

Spare Batteries

P. Thornell, South Gloucestershire

tore. Shorthand thoughts shot through my mind: Are there enough people between us to obscure his vision when he comes out? What hops **READING A** d to duck off? Is anyone helping Kawa **READING A** I had already drawn any countersur- eillar **GOOD BOOK.** notice me now, because before I was hurrying .... rget and now I was taking my time, and people on their way to work don't change their pace that way.

I heard Harry again: 'I'm at one-oh-nine.' Meaning he had turned into the landmark 109 Department Store.

'No good,' I told him. 'The ground floor is lingerie. You going to blend in with teenage girls picking out padded bras?'

'I was planning to wait outside,' he replied, and I could imagine him blushing.

'Just hang back and wait for my signal as we go past,' I said, suppressing the urge to smile.

The fruit store was only ten yards ahead, and still no sign of Kawamura. I could take a chance on just stopping, maybe to fiddle with a cellphone. Still, if he looked, he would spot me standing here, even though, with my father's Japanese features, I don't have problem blending into the crowds. Harry, a pet name for Haruyoshi, being born of two Japanese parents, has never had to worry about sticking out.

10

Waking up just before the alarm goes off

Kirsty Proctor, St Leonards on Sea

... my desk troll.

Hee, hee.

Claire Billesdon, Wiltshire

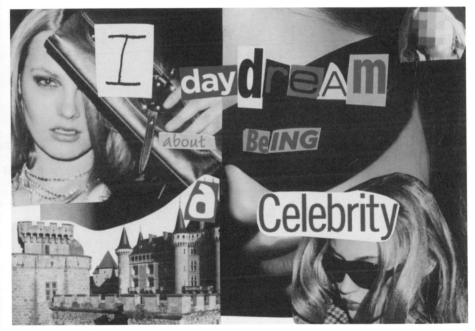

Becki Nolan, Halifax

06. 11. 2005

Anne McCann, by email

In my homeland during a drought, when the red soil is dry beyond dry, the dust feels like baby powder on the bottom of your feet.

Robert Harris, Great Glen

Emma Monkhouse, Chesterfield

Vicky Barron, Braintree

WRITING POETRY - INSTEAD OF DIETING... AGAIN!

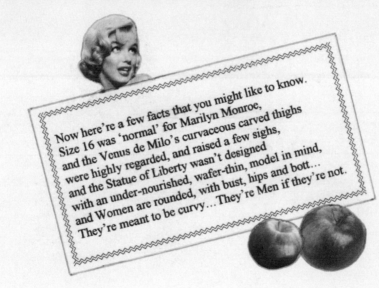

Now here're a few facts that you might like to know.
Size 16 was 'normal' for Marilyn Monroe,
and the Venus de Milo's curvaceous carved thighs
were highly regarded, and raised a few sighs,
and the Statue of Liberty wasn't designed
with an under-nourished, wafer-thin, model in mind,
and Women are rounded, with bust, hips and bott...
They're meant to be curvy... They're Men if they're not.

Nedra Lowe, Chingford

Happiness

Is getting to the top of the
stairs and remembering
what you went up there for.

Patricia Wilson, Lincolnshire

ENTERTAINING FRIENDS
AND WATCHING THEM
ENJOYING THEMSELVES

Here !!
Here !!

M. Burgoyne, Coventry

EMBARRASSING MY CHILDREN

BY SINGING ALONG TO THE MUSIC

Mary Rouncefield, Hotwells

I Love shing Taps and sinks.

Christine Price, Camberley

Sharisse de Silva, Bilston

GETTING
EXCITED
WHEN THE
POST
ARRIVES

Cheryl Connor, Middlesbrough

LOVING MY HUSBAND
WHO AT TIMES I AM
SURE IS SIMPLE

Jennifer Clapet, Grays

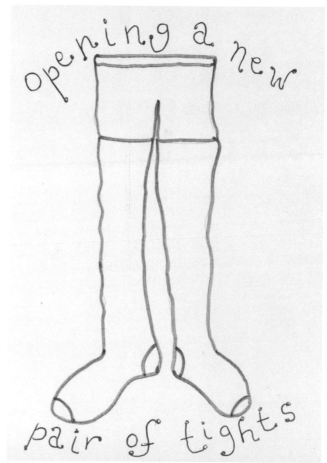

opening a new pair of tights

Deborah Garretty, Leeds

Your stars

TAURUS

21 APR – 21 MAY
Breathe a sigh of relief – Venus is in your sign, and inner tension will be released. It's a magical week for couples because he'll be more assertive. If you're single, be up for a Friday night out with the girls.
★ Your ego gets a boost

hoping for a miracle ......

will it Come true ....

Rita Murphy, Mansfield

Teresa Owen, Northfield

Anonymous, Preston

"HELLO NANNA LUV YOU"

Pat Kemp, Norwich

Paul Frazer, London

Geraldine Coffey, Oldbury

Having enough loo rolls in our bathrooms to pile up as above

Kay Butterworth, Brockenhurst

I Love men who wolfe
whistle, it lifts my spirits

June Herbert, Coventry

Lee Harrall, Ipswich

Vivienne Conlon, Bingley

Having a laugh with my mates over embarrassing pictures of my boyfriend

Allie Jane, Exeter

eating my breakfast standing UP

Kat Harbourne, York

Katie Knott, Staffordshire

DIVORCE
R I P

finding out
there is life after
divorce — a much
better one!!!

LOVE

Jane Ryder, Doncaster

Whenever I'm stressed and things are not going right for me and the whole world seems against me.

When I would turn to my dad to ask for help but know that I can't because he died in 1993.

If I then see a Rainbow I know that whatever is troubling me will sort itself out, as though he has taken the matter out of my hands and sorted it for me. It could be money or a problem at home but it will ALWAYS work out for me.

I know this is my Dad's intervention as at his funeral we had a lovely song played called LOOK FOR ME IN RAINBOWS and that's exactly what I do.

Love you Dad and miss you more than you could ever imagine.

Michelle x

Michelle, by email

Katie & Anne Bronston, Littleover

Jax O'Connor, West Bridgford

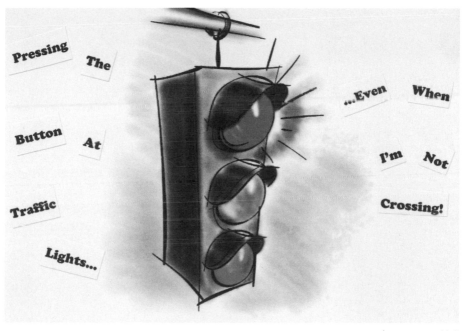

Pressing The Button At Traffic Lights... ...Even When I'm Not Crossing!

Anonymous, Hull

CHIMING CLOCKS -
LOTS OF THEM

Julia Rudkin, West Felton

Bursting the foil
on a new
jar of
Coffee
and being
first
to smell
it......

Heather Paul, West Lothian

I told an old lady at my work
to watch out for our step,
She shouted shed been
"coming here for 30 years,"
she turned around and
fell down the step.

Ruth Hazell, Great Yarmouth

Mandy Buck, Nottingham

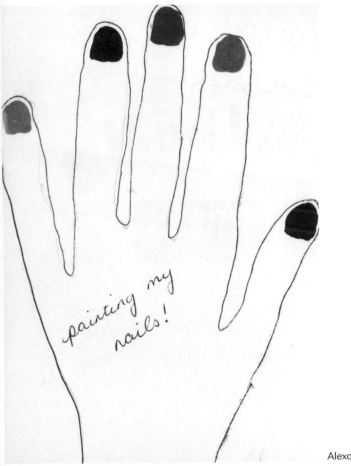

painting my nails!

Alexandra Ford, Fareham

JUMBLING

Fayres and **Wares**

ANTIQUE • FLEA • CAR BOOTS • CRAFT
JUMBLE • TABLE TOP • FETES • ETC

J Jumble Sales

JUMBLE SALE
St Martin's
Church
Fenny Stratford
Sat Feb 11th
11am - 1pm
Admission 20p

ROOSTER CLUTTERBUCK

Sophie Tonks, Milton Keynes

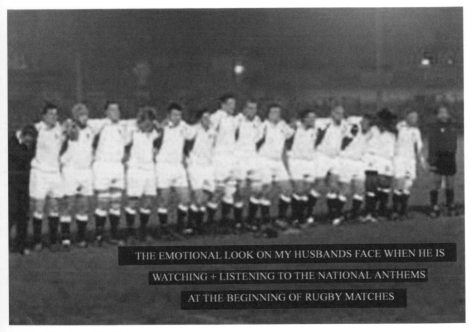

THE EMOTIONAL LOOK ON MY HUSBANDS FACE WHEN HE IS

WATCHING + LISTENING TO THE NATIONAL ANTHEMS

AT THE BEGINNING OF RUGBY MATCHES

Patricia Morrison, Redditch

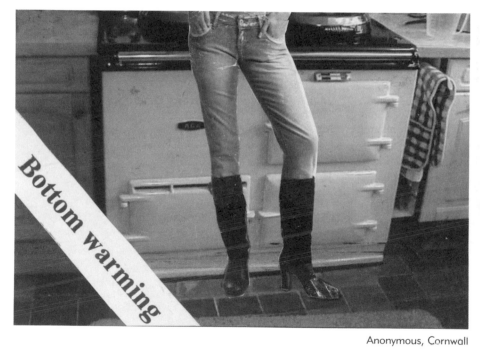

Bottom warming

Anonymous, Cornwall

NO MONEY BUT PLENTY
OF LAUGHS.

Maureen Green, Selkirkshire

Geraldine O'Sullivan, Luton

Emma Cady, Walthamstow

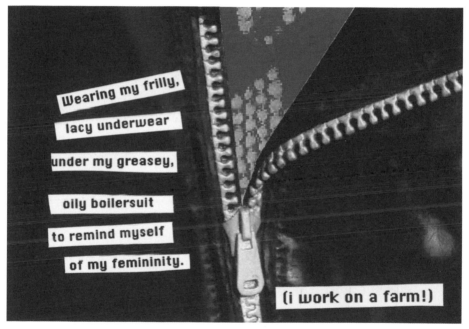

Wearing my frilly, lacy underwear under my greasey, oily boilersuit to remind myself of my femininity.

(i work on a farm!)

D. Smy, Isle of Wight

sending e mails all over the world !!

Pauline Waters, Tyne and Wear

M. Butcher, Norwich